LIGHTNING BOLT BOOKS

It's Windy Today

Kristin Sterling

Lerner Publications Company

To my husband,
Matthew Sterling

Lerner Publications Company
A division of Lerner Publishing Group, Inc.
241 First Avenue North
Minneapolis, MN 55401 U.S.A.

Website address: www.lernerbooks.com

Library of Congress Cataloging-in-Publication Data

Sterling, Kristin.
    It's Windy Today / by Kristin Sterling.
        p.   cm. — (Lightning bolt books™—What's the weather like?)
    Includes index.
    ISBN 978-0-7613-4260-1 (lib. bdg. : alk. paper)
    1. Winds—Juvenile literature. 1. Wind power—Juvenile literature. I. Title.
    QC931.4.S746 2010
    551.518—dc22   2008051582

Manufactured in the United States of America
1 2 3 4 5 6 — BP — 15 14 13 12 11 10

Contents

The Wonder of Wind

Whoosh! The wind blows through a window.

Papers scatter
around the room.
Shutters bang
open and shut.

Wind is moving air. You can
feel wind blowing on your skin.

You can see trees bending and flags flapping in the wind.

Wind makes these colorful wind socks fly.

Wind is caused by warm air rising and cool air falling.

Warm, rising air helps hot air balloons take flight.

Air moves over land and water. It makes waves crash on beaches.

Windy Day Fun

There is so much to do on windy days!

You can fly a kite at the shore.

The wind lifts the kite into the air.

You can blow bubbles. The breeze carries bubbles out of your reach.

You can go sailing on a boat. The wind fills the sails and pushes you across the water.

Sailing is a fun windy-day pastime.

Birds fly using air currents.

Butterflies coast gently in the wind.

Seeds blow away from plants.
Where they land, new plants
will grow.

The wind blows seeds
from this dandelion
into the air.

15

Damaging Winds

Wind moves at different speeds and in different directions.

A gentle breeze makes this wind chime sway.

Slow winds are gentle.
Fast winds can be fierce.

This snowstorm is accompanied by strong winds.

Hurricanes and tornadoes produce fast-moving winds.

Palm tree leaves are scattered on the ground after a storm.

Houses and businesses are damaged. People can get hurt.

A hurricane caused serious damage in this neighborhood.

Sometimes wind knocks over trees and pulls down power lines.

A tree lies on the street after a strong wind knocked it down.

Scientists can help us learn
when storms are coming so
we stay safe.

This scientist tracks a hurricane with the help of computer programs.

Wind Power

Not all fast-moving wind is harmful. Powerful winds can help us too.

This weather vane shows which direction the wind is blowing.

We can
use wind's
power to
light our
homes
and other
buildings.

A scientific
tool measures
wind speed.

Wind turbines capture the power of the wind.

Wind turbines are tall machines with blades. Wind turns their blades around and around.

The turning blades help create electricity. The electricity can be sent to homes to power lights and television sets.

These turbines are on a wind farm—a place where many turbines turn wind into electricity.

25

Another Windy Day

A gentle breeze blows through the window. The wind has died down. Another windy day has ended.

What will you
do on the next
windy day?

Activity
You Can Make an Anemometer

An anemometer is a tool used to measure wind speed. Scientists use them in weather stations. You can make an anemometer with a few simple items.

What you need:
an adult to help you
a marker
four small paper cups
two 10- by 1.5-inch (25.4- by 3.8-centimeter) strips of stiff cardboard
a stapler
a pushpin
a pencil with an eraser
modeling clay

What you do:

1. Use the marker to color the outside of one of the cups.

2. Lay one piece of cardboard over the other in the shape of a **+** sign. Staple them together.

3. Staple the cups to the ends of the cardboard strips. Make sure the cups are all facing the same direction!

4. Push the pin through the middle of the cardboard **+** sign.

5. Push the pencil eraser into the pin.

6. Put a clump of the modeling clay on a flat surface outside. Place the pencil into the clay.

Now you can use your anemometer to measure wind speed. Ask an adult to time you for 1 minute while you count how many times the colored cup goes around in a circle. Write down the number of spins per minute. Try this experiment on several days to see how the wind speed changes.

Glossary

air: a mixture of gases that surrounds Earth

current: air that moves continuously in a certain direction

hurricane: a strong storm with high winds that often starts in the Atlantic Ocean

tornado: a whirling column of air that appears as a cloud shaped like a funnel

wind: moving air

wind turbine: a machine that captures the power of the wind. Wind turbines help turn wind power into electricity.

Further Reading

Dorros, Arthur. *Feel the Wind.* New York: Crowell, 1989.

Energy Kid's Page: Wind Energy
http://www.eia.doe.gov/kids/energyfacts/sources/renewable/wind.html

FEMA for Kids: Hurricanes
http://www.fema.gov/kids/hurr.htm

Malone, Peter. *Close to the Wind: The Beaufort Scale.* New York: G. P. Putnam's Sons, 2007.

Marsico, Katie. *Windy Weather Days.* New York: Children's Press, 2007.

Sterling, Kristin. *It's Cloudy Today.* Minneapolis: Lerner Publications Company, 2010.

Index

Photo Acknowledgments

The images in this book are used with the permission of: © Yetis/iStockphoto.com/
Cindy Singleton, p. 1; © iStockphoto.com/Susan Stewart, p. 2; © Felipe Dupouy/Getty
Images, p. 4; © Christian Hoehm/Stone/Getty Images, p. 5; © iStockphoto.com/Felix
Mizioznikov, p. 6; © iStockphoto.com/Ian Stewart, p. 7; © Jim Lozouski/Shutterstock
Images, p. 8; © Galyna Andrushko/Shutterstock Images, p. 9; © iStockphoto.com/
Deborah Cheramie, p. 10; © iStockphoto.com/Michael van den Brink, p. 11; © iStock-
photo.com/mohamed sadath, p. 12; © iStockphoto.com/Loretta Hostettler, p. 13;
© iStockphoto.com/Diane Diederich, p. 14; © Bidouze Stephane/Shutterstock Images,
p. 15; © Tohoku Color Agency/Japan Images/Getty Images, p. 16; © Stephen Wilkes/
Stone/Getty Images, p. 17; © Stockphoto.com/ROBERTO ADRIAN, p. 18; © Visions LLC/
Photolibrary, p. 19; © Radius Images/Photolibrary, p. 20; © Joe Raedle/Getty Images,
p. 21; © Flirt/SuperStock, p. 22; © Suzanne Long/Photolibrary, p. 23; © Stuart Pearce/
Photolibrary, p. 24; © Yekorzh/Dreamstime.com, p. 25; © Fancy Collection/SuperStock,
p. 26; © iStockphoto.com/Aldo Murillo, p. 27; © Todd Strand/Independent Picture
Service, p. 28; © Digital Vision/Getty Images, p. 30; © Loop Delay/Westend61/
Photolibrary, p. 31.

Front cover: © iStockphoto.com/Oscar Gutierrez.